Bb

Warren Rylands and Eric Doty

www.av2books.com

LET'S READ AV² BY WEIGL™
ADDED VALUE • AUDIO VISUAL

Go to **www.av2books.com**, and enter this book's unique code.

BOOK CODE

K 6 2 8 8 4 6

AV² by Weigl brings you media enhanced books that support active learning.

AV² provides enriched content that supplements and complements this book. Weigl's AV² books strive to create inspired learning and engage young minds in a total learning experience.

Your AV² Media Enhanced books come alive with...

 Audio
Listen to sections of the book read aloud.

 Video
Watch informative video clips.

 Embedded Weblinks
Gain additional information for research.

Try This!
Complete activities and hands-on experiments.

 Key Words
Study vocabulary, and complete a matching word activity.

 Quizzes
Test your knowledge.

 Slide Show
View images and captions, and prepare a presentation.

... and much, much more!

Published by AV² by Weigl
350 5th Avenue, 59th Floor
New York, NY 10118

Website: www.av2books.com

Library of Congress Control Number: 2015940604

ISBN 978-1-4896-3471-9 (hardcover)
ISBN 978-1-4896-3473-3 (single user eBook)
ISBN 978-1-4896-3474-0 (multi-user eBook)

Printed in the United States of America in Brainerd, Minnesota
1 2 3 4 5 6 7 8 9 0 19 18 17 16 15

052015
WEP050815

Project Coordinator: Katie Gillespie   Art Director: Terry Paulhus

Weigl acknowledges Getty Images and iStock as the primary image suppliers for this title.

Bb

CONTENTS

Let's explore the letter

The uppercase letter **B**
looks like this

The lowercase letter **b**
looks like this

The letter b can start many words.

bird

ball

balloon

banana

bear

7

The letter b can be inside a word.

bubble

bum**b**le**b**ee

to**b**oggan

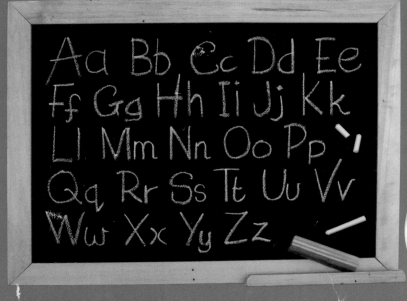

blac**k**board

9

The letter **b** can be at the end of a word.

cra**b**

climb

cab

cob

lab

11

Many names start with an uppercase B.

Beth

Bruce plays soccer.

Brenda can fly.

Ben likes rockets.

Brian gives thumbs up.

13

The letter **b** can make a sound or stay quiet.

boy

thumb

The letter **b**  makes a sound in the word boy.

 The letter **b** does not make a sound in the word thumb.

15

The letter **b** makes a sound in most words.

be

back

web

about

job

17

Sometimes the letter **b** does not make a sound.

lamb

numb

plumber

crumb

comb

19

Having Fun with B

Bob is a big blue bird.

He likes big balloons and bouncy basketball balls.

Bob's friend Brent the black bear loves basketball too.

Who is better between Bob and Brent?

Brent can play backward and barefoot!

But Bob can bolt fast and breeze by Brent.

Both are bright and brave boys.

The alphabet
has 26 letters.

B is the second letter
in the alphabet.

Aa **Bb** Cc Dd **Ee**

Ff **Gg** Hh Ii Jj Kk

Ll **Mm** Nn Oo Pp

Qq Rr Ss Tt Uu Vv

Ww Xx Yy Zz

23

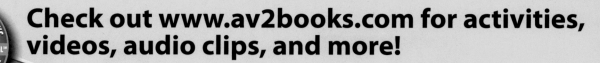

Bb

24